*Brief Candles*

# Brief Candles

## 101 CLERIHEWS

*For Wenid* (handwritten)

## HENRY TAYLOR

*With all best wishes,* (handwritten signature and date)

*9/25/03* (handwritten)

*Folger* (handwritten)

*Louisiana State University Press  Baton Rouge*

MM

Copyright © 1999, 2000 by Henry Taylor
Illustrations copyright © 2000 by Heather Alexander
All rights reserved
Manufactured in the United States of America
First printing
09  08  07  06  05  04  03  02  01  00
5   4   3   2   1

Designer: Michele Myatt Quinn
Typeface: Bembo
Printer and binder: Thomson-Shore, Inc.

Library of Congress Cataloging-in-Publication Data
Taylor, Henry, 1942–
        Brief candles : 101 Clerihews / Henry Taylor.
        p. cm.
        ISBN 0-8071-2563-6 (cloth : alk. paper)—ISBN 0-8071-
2564-4 (pbk. : alk. paper)
        1. Clerihews. 2. Biography—Poetry. 3. Humorous
poetry, American. I. Title.

PS3570.A93 B74 2000
811'.54—dc21
                                                    99-055345

The author is grateful to the editors of the following publica-
tions, in which some of the poems herein first appeared: Book-
list, Gargoyle, Goose Creek News, Maine Times, and New York Times
Book Review. The "Readers in Theory" clerihews appeared in
the internet magazine Cortland Review.

The paper in this book meets the guidelines for permanence
and durability of the Committee on Production Guidelines for
Book Longevity of the Council on Library Resources. ∞

David Slavitt and William Jay Smith
have been friends, inspirers, and joys to be with.
Therefore, this book, if they will have it,
is for William Jay Smith and David Slavitt.

# Contents

# Acknowledgments

My favorite pages here are Heather Alexander's; her drawings have caught the tone and mood of this book more thoroughly than I would have thought possible.

I am also grateful to the Virginia Commission for the Arts, for a fellowship that enabled me to complete this collection, and to the staff of the Hawthorne-Longfellow Library at Bowdoin College, for the untiring graciousness with which they assist visitors.

These verses emerged from a brief but difficult period, and were an odd but powerful aid in the maintenance of my equilibrium. For the maintenance of my physical well-being during that time, I am forever indebted to Drs. Kin-Sing Au, Keith Belote, Theodore Corcoran, Lewis Estabrooks, Carlton Fairbanks, Deidre Bird Kokel, David Moyer, and Rangappa Rajendra, as well as to the many therapeutic and administrative staff members in their offices, especially Punam Dutt and Carol Gavin. My gratitude to friends and family is beyond measure or expression.

# Prologue: Clerihew

Edmund C. Bentley
let his middle name fall gently
upon this short verse form. Perhaps he
foresaw the case of Adelaide Crapsey.

# I

## JUST FOR A RIBAND

### The British Poets Laureate

John Dryden
wasn't the sort you'd confide in;
there was no limit to the secrets he'd tell
in lyrics set to music by Henry Purcell.


Thomas Shadwell
kept a notebook in which he had well
over three dozen rhymes for "toad."
He originated the Birthday Ode.


Nahum Tate
may have been second-rate,
but a mighty boost to his career
was his happy ending for *King Lear.*


Nicholas Rowe
always knew where to go;
people who rode with him often said
he must have had a map of London in his head.


Laurence Eusden
is said to have abused an
embarrassing quantity of sack;
it got so bad people quit keeping track.

Colley Cibber
was an inveterate ribber;
he'd ring up Dean Swift on the telephone
and do a flawless impression of the Stone of Scone.


William Whitehead
was not knighted
for facing *The Dangers of Writing Verse;*
over the years he got steadily worse.


Thomas Warton
never met Dolly Parton.
It made him quite surly
to have been born too early.


Henry James Pye
is extremely difficult to justify;
none of the writing he managed to do
has been reprinted since 1822.


Robert Southey
took neither bearing nor azimuth.  He
liked to say
that he could just feel his way.

William Wordsworth
considered four and twenty birds worth
a walk as far as the banks of the Wye.
There are some things money just can't buy.

Alfred, Lord Tennyson,
once solved an enigma: when is an
eider most like a merganser?
He lived long enough to forget the answer.

Alfred Austin
could get lost in
his own backyard
and took most things too hard.

Robert Bridges
lived into the era of fridges
but doubted they were worth their price.
He hadn't much use for ice.

The ghost of John Masefield
intensely surveys field
and wood, even looks under rocks
for the vanishing fur-flame of Reynard the Fox.

C. Day Lewis
understood what a clue is;
whenever one of them kept him awake
he'd write another novel by Nicholas Blake.


Sir John Betjeman
was not at all an edgy man;
relaxed, remote, he loved to pose
in Henry James's morning clothes.


Ted Hughes
had an ear for bad news,
but his intenser flights apart,
he was a meat-and-potatoes fellow at heart.


Andrew Motion
could make moisturizing lotion.
Much of what he now creates
is slick and fragrant, and evaporates.

# II

A. Alvarez
came to know what bizarre is;
he found himself feeling so odd
he sat down and wrote

## THE SAVAGE GOD

Lucan
took an
elegant knife,
opened a vein and bled out his life.


Eustace Budgell
found that writing pure sludge'll
earn a few lines in Pope's *Dunciad*.
He's lost the luster that once he had.


Thomas Chatterton
shunned being spattered on;
he helped himself to some arsenic
and kept his cadaver more scenic.


Vladimir Mayakovsky
was scornful of golf club, of kayak, of ski,
and of sporty aristocrats who let
poor poets lose at Russian roulette.


Hart Crane
plunged into the bounding main.
His situation could not have been graver:
his father invented the *candy* Lifesaver.

Cesare Pavese
didn't exactly go crazy,
but suffered forty-two years
with vague, powerful fears.

Vachel Lindsay
heard the wind say
there's a time to die
and took a big swig of lye.

Sylvia Plath
trod a difficult path
more on than in the shoes
of Ted Hughes.

Into the traffic Randall Jarrell
jumped, stumbled, or fell
while sane, drugged, or delirious:
it's mysterious.

Richard Brautigan
couldn't catch the rich trout again
so he turned toward the haywire harms
of alcohol and firearms.

Paul Celan
tried to revive his vital élan,
but the attempt being vain
he jumped into the Seine.


John Berryman
hailed the grim ferryman
at a point from which his descent could be reckoned
at thirty-two feet per second per second.


Lew Welch
failed to squelch
the little voice inside that said
he ought to shoot himself in the head.


Weldon Kees
parked by a bridge and rode the breeze.
It would be better by far
to have found Kees in the car.

# III

## Disciples

Peter,
the official greeter,
administrates
the Pearly Gates.


Peter's brother Andrew,
in a strange blend of devotion and rue,
let his nets drop from his hand
and left them there upon the sand.


James the son of Zebedee
preferred to be
known as the Greater; "Yet may God bless,"
he said, "my colleague, James the Less."


The son of Alphaeus, called James,
nursed a variety of lofty aims,
but was endowed by his Creator
with due respect for James the Greater.


John
believed on the Son,
ate the bread of life,
and avoided strife.

Thomas,
though given to psychodramas,
found nothing up the Savior's sleeve
and came to believe.

Jude,
an intense kind of dude,
wrote an epistle brief but dire
warning us all of eternal fire.

Philip
drank from the cup with the nonspill lip
when Jesus found him in Galilee
and sent him to look under the fig tree.

Bartholomew,
hearing from afar a hollow moo,
said to himself, "That'll
be Nineveh thriving: also much cattle."

According to Matthew
the wrath you
flee may be your own:
live not by bread alone.

Simon
was hardly a shy man.
When his mother-in-law had a fever
he brought Jesus to relieve her.

Judas Iscariot
missed the sweet chariot
but swung pretty low
in his wasteland of woe.

Matthias
gave discipleship a try as
the last-minute result
of betrayal and tumult.

*Entr'acte*

Adelaide Crapsey
induces narcolepsy:
most of her cinquains
fade as invisible ink wanes.


Louis Pasteur
kept his libido astir
by pretending to disrobe
in the presence of a microbe.


Said Dame Edith Sitwell,
"This hat doesn't fit well.
Since I already have several,
try this one on Sacheverell."


Tommaso Landolfi
was disdainful of golf. He
considered putting
more vulgar than rutting.


Preston Sturges
was subject to urges
whose nature and history
remain shrouded in mystery.

# IV

## READERS IN THEORY

Harold Bloom,
the crack of doom,
and the loggerhead shrike
are much alike.


Noam Chomsky
worked over such phrases as "bum ski"
and "ski bum," applying generative grammar
and a ballpeen hammer.


Hélène Cixous,
she who
speaks of discourse as clitoral,
is not being literal.


Jacques Derrida
forgot where he'd—ah,
then he remembered:
deconstructed need not mean dismembered.


Michel Foucault
made a wicked osso buco.
As the veal shin-bones began to turn brownish,
you could hear him crooning, "Discipline and punish."

Gérard Genette
poached a few tropes in his kitchenette.
There hadn't been such a mélange of rhetorics
since Caesar engaged with Vercingetorix.


bell hooks,
when she gets funny looks
about lowercase letters, likes to wrap it all
up by exclaiming, "first-rate! splendid! capital!"


Paul de Man
never drove at Le Mans.
He was found to have published reprehensible views
concerning Jews.


Camille Paglia
believes feminist folly a
splendid occasion
for sarcastical suasion.


Ferdinand de Saussure
sometimes lost his composure
when expounding his dream of the structural whole
underlying the laws of *langue* and *parole.*

# V

## READERS IN PRACTICE

Calvin Bedient
lacks an ingredient
that he keeps in a squirt
bottle under his shirt.

Sven Birkerts!
Sometimes his work hurts,
but at least he doesn't jerk us
around like Virginia Kirkus.

Alan Cheuse
airs his views
while with guarded stares
we view his airs.

Michael Dirda
's pretty weird: a
reader who takes many a hint
from antique books long out of print.

Paul Gray
remains above the fray,
the scandal, the innuendo, and the grime
that appear in *Time*.

Doris Grumbach's
boom box
plays the blues
to mixed reviews.


Michiko Kakutani
often tests bombs, but is not Pakistani;
her ancestry, if you please,
is Japanese.


Christopher Lehmann-Haupt
exquisitely yawped
in accents most humanitarian:
he doesn't even *read* Barbarian.

> A nameless but punctilious hysteric
> reminds me that *barbaric*
> is the original text.
> A valid point, well taken. Thank you. Next?


Carol Muske
had a husky
style
for a while.

Peter S. Prescott
got up to dress, caught
his flesh in his zipper,
and became Jack the Ripper.


Richard Tillinghast,
absorbed in painkilling, gassed
not only himself
but the entire Five-Foot Shelf.


Helen Vendler
slant rhymes with handler, swindler, fondler, and trundler.
So why get out the crying towel
over the commonest English vowel?


Jonathan Yardley
reads softly but writes hardly,
beating the bounds of his dominion
over matters purely of opinion.

*Entr'acte*

George Fox
was heedless of clocks;
he attended in silence on the Word,
then rose and spoke at length of what he'd heard.


Friedrich Nietzsche
strove vainly to reach a
steadfast decision
between Apollonian and Dionysian.


Jerry Falwell
may not think at all well
but has done some sharp dealing
with organized feeling.


Ann Landers
never panders
and Abigail van Buren
has no dope in her urine.


Samuel Taylor Coleridge
would take his stick and stroll a ridge,
having left his study door locked
to keep his poems from being Porlocked.

Alexander Graham Bell
has shuffled off this mobile cell.
He's not talking any more,
but he has a lot to answer for.

# VI

## WATERS WHITE, MURKY, AND OTHERWISE

President Clinton
might be tempted to stint on
the legal expenses
of ill-mended fences.


Henry Hyde
struggled to decide
what the truth was
and when his youth was.


Gennifer Flowers
has unusual powers
of attraction, and charm in generous amounts.
It is sobering to see just how much spelling counts.


Susan McDougal
may have been less than frugal
with the household funds of Zubin Mehta,
or she may be the object of a vendetta.


Linda Tripp
has a view of friendship
in which loyal trust is
obstruction of justice.

Should Robert Pinsky
meet Monica Lewinsky
he'd surely give her no
lip; just his version of *The Inferno.*

Monica Lewinsky,
upon encountering Robert Pinsky,
probably wouldn't ask him home,
but might recite her favorite pome.

Webster Hubbell
went to a great deal of trouble
to keep the President free from stain.
He might have to do it again.

# VII

## The High Bench

William Rehnquist
grew testy when quizzed
concerning how sober
a judge ought to be the first week in October.

Stephen Breyer,
when a tabloid called to inquire
whether he is a space alien,
felt sure of his status as earthly mammalian.

Ruth Bader Ginsburg
said *Titanic,* in truth, made her wince. "Berg
phobia?" asked a reporter.
"No," she said, "I just wish it were shorter."

Anthony Kennedy
was startled: when had he
removed his tie?
And why?

Sandra Day O'Connor
was just about to don her
robes when her clerk
simply went berserk.

Antonin Scalia
likes to sing "The Rose of Tralee"—a
treat for all students
of his jurisprudence.


David Souter
booted up his computer
and discovered that sex is
treated drily on LEXIS.


John Paul Stevens
is one of the evens
against the odds, standing unbent
by his dissent.


Clarence Thomas
preserved and protected his early promise
by making sure he never strayed
into discussions of *Roe v. Wade.*

## Epilogue: Cold War Closure

Nikita Khrushchev,
bodiless as loose chaff,
within a narrow clerihew
there's room at last to bury you.

## GOOD NEWS
*by Lee Smith*

Henry Taylor
(older, paler)
now has joined those merry few
devoted to the clerihew!